GIFTS TO SHARE

Volume II

JAMES SHIELDS

To Rosita. My wife, My friend, My muse.

Acknowledgements

Many thanks to Cleda Flener for her unwavering support and assistance!

Special thanks to my amazing sister, Marie Summers! You have believed in me and supported my writing from the beginning!

1

There is a song *success* sings from the heart…
Falls from the lips of those who do rejoice,
Who stayed the course, beginning at the start,
Would not surrender to surrender's voice.

Held firm in darkness of the darkest night,
Ignored naysayers when they shook their heads,
Convinced beyond a doubt his path was right,
He chose to ponder *positives* instead.

While others may not fully understand,
Believing his achievements followed fate,
Ignoring that each step was fully planned;
Attainment favors those who will not wait.

Hard work and perseverance brought him through…
The hardest part of doing is the *do*.

2

Confused I am by what some people do,
They think that everyone should always win;
Most every sport and every game they skew,
Act as if losing is some kind of sin.

Sincere they are, I'm sure, in what they try…
Convinced defeat contributes to the strife,
Believing loss brings damage by and by,
Destroying chances for a happy life.

While I applaud their efforts and concerns,
I wonder if they've really thought this out…
Accepting loss is how young folks will learn;
In life sometimes we fail, sometimes we shout.

Participation trophies will conceal;
Winners and losers are what keep life real.

3

So I asked *death*, who does he think he is,
Here acting like he won the game and all…
As he struts around in ignorant bliss,
Oblivious that he fell with the fall.

He thinks his team puts points up on the board,
Believing he's about to win the game,
Forgetting his big fight here with the Lord…
Since then, death's power hasn't been the same.

Just like his boss, he whispers futile lies,
Pretending he has all things in control…
Suggesting still he doesn't realize
His piddling power cannot touch man's soul.

He makes a lot of noise with all his friends,
They're helpless to change how the story ends!

4

It isn't that we've chosen not to care…
Although some folks are now convinced we've failed.
Questioning time-tempered thoughts many share,
Unwilling to accept the ship has sailed.

I'll be among the first to stand and say
Our ancestors destroyed all moral ground…
Beyond good sense, they overlooked the ways
Cruel men abused the human lives they found.

For though I was not present at that time
And never would condone those awful things,
I still emphatically deplore the crimes
With all abhorrent sequelae it brings.

No words can ever make slavery be right,
And I most willingly will hold a light!

5

The oak leaves have been brushed in snowy white…
Smooth meadow edges now outlined as though
The painter of all nature got it right
When He stopped by, His handiwork to show.

A cold north wind reminds me it is here,
Its chilly fingers sting me to the bone;
I'm hoping that my animals are near.
The sun begins to set. I am alone.

I walk into the shadows of the moon…
The ones I've come to fetch follow my bell.
The path seems long, I'll see my homeplace soon;
I know my love is watching, I can tell.

The night is young, I know more snow will fall;
I listen on the wind, I hear her call!

6

We watched a shooting star streak through the sky,
Amazed at the sheer beauty of it all...
Tucked inside our blanket, my love and I,
Before the summer's end, a taste of fall.

Cool evening air, a respite from the sun,
Fireflies bring a soft lightning serenade.
When flashing in the darkness is all done...
We're grateful for the beauty here displayed.

Some day when time has ceased being our friend,
These memories we share will hold us near,
Reminding us this night need never end...
Placed with each recollection we hold dear.

Never a wasted time or wasted space,
Each day collecting moments to embrace.

7

Efficiently, the spider weaves his art…
It glistens in the early morning dew,
Begun before my day could even start,
His masterpiece will tempt more than a few.

So clever and quite plan-refined is he…
His prey will rarely realize he's there,
Just waiting in his corner patiently
Appears he is asleep, without a care.

Then soon a single wasp came buzzing by,
Alerting Master Spider of his guest;
Eventually, the bee will cease to try…
He will not be returning to his nest.

I watch them as the victor moves to eat…
In spiders *justified* - in men *deceit*.

8

One dark night recently I had a dream…
It seemed to last for hours, maybe more;
Quite shocked I was, how real a dream could seem,
Leads me to question what it might be for.

Could be the meal I had too close to bed,
Maybe something I've viewed lodged in my brain,
Perhaps the remnants of what someone said,
Just coming back to stir my thoughts again.

Or maybe it was really heaven-sent,
Celestial waves beyond our atmosphere…
So hard to say what it might represent,
Just what they may want me to know down here.

I'm overcome, the wonder of it all…
Too bad there's not one frame I can recall.

9

For years it stood upon the hill, a shrine,
Dark branches outstretched like a lover's reach,
Providing solace from the bright sunshine…
Such lessons in endurance it could teach.

Steadfastly watched travelers on their way,
A sapling when the red man then roamed free,
Saw herds of buffalo back in their day,
When folks saw nature as nature should be.

The years rolled past and change was everywhere…
The path became a road, became a street;
Ten thousand busy folks passed by it there,
But being just a tree could not compete.

No doubt it weathered countless storms before…
Until the one last night, now it's no more.

10

They do the things they do because they can,
This band of thugs and miscreants et al.
Defacing precious artifacts—their plan,
Convinced they're answering some higher call.

Their stealth for opportunity is clear…
Small swarms attacking much like angry bees;
Then, fueled by some commitment they hold dear,
They vandalize just when and where they please.

Misguided actions rarely do succeed,
Creating outrage well beyond their plan,
Which drives away support they clearly need;
They play their games, then lose and lose again.

Their lack of wisdom ought to give them pause…
Such foolishness will not enhance their cause.

11

Windswept and weathered, waiting for the rain,
Dry and dusty, sun-drenched, discarded fields…
Forgotten farm, if it could feel, then pain,
What years of wasted worthlessness will yield.

Though never *Edenesque* for all we know,
Providing crops enough for folks to eat…
Among the weeds and wanting, they would grow
Until all was surrendered to defeat.

Just tossed aside until folks found a way
To send cool water from the lakes nearby…
Now seems the grass grows greener every day,
Soft breeze flows through the fields, a lullaby.

This land transformed into a showplace here
Should make our path to help others more clear.

12

The faintest glow can tame the darkest night
It inspires and gives me hope within…
It has no thoughts to share of wrong or right,
When one should stop, or when they should begin.

Maybe the light's affixed to someone's door,
Placed there by faith, inviting shadows warm,
Or high upon a tower shining more,
Intended to guide us away from harm.

I walk in peace toward that distant glow…
The darkness will not slow my steady pace,
For somewhere deep inside my heart I know
I'll find what I am seeking in that place.

Some day when life recalls this memory…
How I pray someone else's light to be.

13

Because there is no water on the moon,
It surely is a dry and dusty place;
I don't think that will change any time soon…
Besides, we're all accustomed to its face.

I do suppose it would be fun to see,
When looking skyward on a starry night,
A patch of bushy bushes or a tree…
But somehow that just does not seem quite right.

So many jobs we know it's charged to do,
Just sitting in the sky and all alone…
Beyond just shining down on me and you,
All with so little gratitude it's shown.

We've known *different's* not *better* all along…
Change for the sake of *changing* can be wrong.

14

Elephants were dancing in the moonlight;
The chimpanzees were swinging to and fro.
Lions were parading like it's all right,
To let their hair hang down a bit, you know.

The zebras heard music and came running,
While cockatoos all tried to sing their song;
Tigers were dismayed at all the *funning*,
The hippos just refused to go along.

The leopard screamed, he was so excited,
The others let him know that was not fine.
The lizard sulked, he was not invited,
For creepy-crawly things they drew the line.

That dream I had reminded me, it's true...
Wild beasts can't get along like people do!

15

Each person has their own reason to play…
For some, it simply is a get-rich deal,
While others think it takes hurting away,
With hope and dreams that rarely become real.

They say you have to play to win, that's true…
While quietly, it takes what we will earn;
The odds of winning ought to be a clue.
Still, folks continue playing when they learn.

We read of all the good it claims it's done…
No doubt it does a little now and then;
Though seems a curse to many who have won,
Yet some still feel the need to play again.

With promises of *grandiosity*,
It preys upon what poor folks wish to be.

16

I'm told that if the sunshine were to end…
Eight minutes later, folks would start to feel
An absence of the warmth it always sends,
When chilling darkness began to be real.

How long it's been up there, no one can know…
The warm light we enjoy, fair Eden knew,
It lit the tree and helped the fruit to grow
That brought about the demise of those two.

But still, it keeps on doing what it does…
It's never faltered, never changed at all;
We have no need to think about what was,
Before God placed that giant yellow ball.

While men and science debate what's ahead,
Wise folks will simply walk in light instead.

17

Sometimes the enemy gets on a roll,
Then does his best to make me start to doubt
There is a destination for my soul,
Or anything that God is all about.

There have been times when he would try to say
Religion's just for those who cannot cope,
They just use faith to guide them when they pray
In situations when they have no hope.

At times he tries to get me to believe
Intelligence does not allow such things,
To make me question the gifts I receive,
Including joy and peace that faith will bring.

So... here is my assessment of it all:
If God's not real, then why would Satan call?

18

The snow is falling onto frozen ground,
Seems storm last night decided it would stay;
I'm standing here enjoying morning sounds,
As forest prepares for another day.

White-coated branches sway now overhead,
The cold air pushes them in gentle stride;
They groan as if they would prefer instead
To pass on winter and just live inside.

It's such a blessing for me to be here,
To leave my worried, hurried world behind…
Maybe this calm will help my mind to clear,
A brief and tranquil peace perhaps to find.

This busy life can take more than it gives…
Here in this place, I'm reassured He lives.

19

I've walked around this mountain my last time,
Been here so long it should now have my name.
Lies I believed make no reason or rhyme,
If I am here, or I am there, the same.

The giants stole my joy and strength somehow,
I tried ignoring them to no avail.
I've decided it will be over now,
Too long I've been a ship without a sail.

But that all changes here for me today!
I've heard the truth, that by His grace I'm free!
I'm so alive, by faith I've walked away,
No more a life of servitude for me!

So many times, I've had to run and hide...
Now ever in His shadow, I'll abide!

20

Two folks lost in a dark and dismal wood,
Midnight found them exhausted and distraught;
Just fumbling there without water or food,
They could not find deliverance they sought.

The night was cold but they refused to quit,
Quite sure their path was somewhere waiting there;
Each knew the challenge they faced finding it,
Obscured by leaves still blowing in the air.

But then, as they were stumbling all about,
Sunlight began reflecting all around...
Redemption had arrived for them no doubt!
It came with softest touch, without a sound.

When night has stolen all our hope away...
How small problems can look in light of day!

21

Where was the joy they promised me that day…
So long I'd been there, waiting for the call,
Seemed all that I held dear was washed away,
Just syncopated sunlight, if at all.

Surrendered to their skillful, well-placed plans,
I fell in line with every rule and law,
Convinced me then that the best course was man's,
Instructed to accept all that I saw.

They chose their one to rule over the rest,
Said God would speak to him, but not to me;
Finally though, I knew they'd missed God's best,
Those who remained there never would be free.

He made a way, I've left it all behind!
I'm praying now that He will heal my mind.

22

Who then could ever know the eagle's course…
She rides on crystal breezes men can't see!
There in her world she's such an awesome force,
A life unshackled to humanity.

High in a rocky cleft, she builds her nest…
The mate she finds will be her only one.
At no point does she fear a season's test,
A team of equals, as all work gets done.

They soar a mile or two above the ground,
Then ride the currents as they rise and fall…
Cold silence softened by their distant sounds…
A *symphony in motion* says it all.

The eagle is a wonder to behold…
No greater nature's story has been told!

23

It seems to me God's criticized too much…
Gets blamed for many things He did not do,
As though He has destruction in His touch,
When often those to blame are me and you.

Folks make poor choices each and every day…
Wild things adults do, all in having fun,
Drive everything in every which-a-way;
Quite often someone's hurting when they're done.

We all know kids with matches can get burned,
Yet, parents step right up to go along…
By now it seems the lessons would be learned,
But then claim it was God that got it wrong.

God promises salvation now to man…
It's too bad common sense escapes His plan.

24

High above the windswept meadow she flies,
This graceful ballerina in the air…
Strong currents cause her now to realize,
She's drifted from the small ones in her care.

Up there she leaves the endless earth behind,
Now silent solitude a welcomed choice;
Soon she will turn upwind again to find
New generations listening for her voice!

Then flying home, she'll capture dinner's feast,
Ensuring every hungry mouth gets fed;
She'll touch each one, the largest to the least,
Could leave them, yes, but chooses here instead.

Real parenting involves commitment, true…
A natural course, people should follow too!

25

Folks wonder what he was back in the day,

Before the years began to steal his light.

Perhaps a leader of men, who could say,

Back when folks knew much more of wrong and right.

They watched him from a distance, watched his ways,

Him staring quite alone as if to find

Some part of memory that chose to stay,

Things time has taken, yet has left behind.

So much that he has seen but cannot share;

Some wish that they had known him way back when…

The distance in his eyes shows he's been where

Men pray to never have to pass again.

Folks whisper in his presence, and I see

The old man they're discussing here, is me.

26

Please don't say you want to doubt creation…
So many doubters I have met before;
Patiently, I provide explanations,
But seems like some folks always ask for more.

Truth is, God made it so easy to see…
Such evidence He's been willing to share
To prove He's everything He claims to be,
With grace enough for all, and some to spare.

Yet, some folks still refuse to let Him in
Until each question's answered, when they call;
But faith is where each person must begin,
And faith from seeing's - not real faith at all.

He wants to be a part of all we do…
Wise men still seek Him, that we know, is true.

27

The old spring, hidden well beneath the bluff,
A Godsend to our family back then;
Its water very cold and pure enough,
It served our homeplace time and time again.

Each morning when the air was crisp and still,
The children took their empty buckets down
That rocky, leaf-strewn path below the hill
Where life-sustaining treasure could be found.

Seems no one gave much thought about its source,
Or how it could pass freely through the stones,
Or how it was directed on its course
To serve no other family but our own.

We never let those things we did not know
Cause us to miss the way His blessings flow!

28

There, among the first things I remember
From when we moved out to the old homeplace…
Remnants of a chilly late November,
Fond memories that cannot be erased.

Each evening when the sun was setting low
We'd light the oil lamps to help us see,
Then watch the shadows dancing in their glow…
Each child's imagination running free.

Clear summer nights, when weather warmed a bit,
We'd gather on the porch to watch the lights,
As fireflies performed their graceful skits…
A simple prayer before we said goodnight.

Our lives shared stories that old porch could bring…
Learning to trust God for everything.

29

We heard a storm was coming late that night,
Seemed mostly they would come when we're asleep;
The weather folks don't always get it right,
But that time they predicted water deep!

Rain started falling as the darkness came…
And really didn't look too bad at first;
In fact, so many storms had looked the same,
We saw no need preparing for the worst.

Pa sent us all to bed with little fear…
We said a prayer the water wouldn't rise;
He woke us yelling, "Let's get out of here!"
The river had raised up to twice its size!

We thought God did not hear our prayers no more…
And yet the river never touched our door!

30

Then I saw a red and threatening sky,
Cloud layers framed the deepest, darkest part…
Concerned and frightened by the scene was I,
There seemed to be no ending and no start!

The air I breathed was hot and full of life,
Creating dusty spinners all around;
They filled my space with caution and with strife,
As each one skipped the bone-dry, barren ground.

Just what it all might mean, I could not say…
I sensed a storm was coming to that place;
And though I hoped that it would go away,
It did not all the fear in me erase.

I hunkered down until the storm was through…
For what else could a tiny church mouse do?

31

The elephant was large and scary too,

Just tethered to a small stake in the dirt;

The folks there were aware what he could do…

Full knowing - that if free, he could cause hurt.

Truth is, his owners knew he wouldn't try,

It was not magic or some kind of spell;

They thought it good for folks to wonder why…

It helped their business grow, best they could tell.

For when the elephant was very small,

The owners tied it to large blocks of stone;

Those anchors would not let it stray at all.

It can't forget the past now that it's grown.

The poet Wordsworth seemed to understand,

He wrote, "*The child is father to the man.*"

32

If all the stuff we own were made of ice,
It would not last too very long… therefore,
We'd never hear our family's advice
To clear things out before we go get more.

We would not feel the need for extra space,
Things would look nice, then quickly fade away…
There'd be no reason to join in the race
To justify how much we had to pay.

Maybe it would help us appreciate
The blessings that we have before they're gone…
Be thankful for each gift before too late,
Instead of marking time as it moves on.

Perhaps my thoughts may cause some folks to smile,
Accumulating more stuff all the while.

33

Far-reaching is the hand of love, it seems,
When incident or happenstance brings pain,
Cause hearts to overflow when needs they deem
To make the wounded life whole once again.

We hear sad tales of those who find a way
To add more sadness as their sole intent,
Through hurtful actions and cruel words they say,
As if their good had long ago been spent.

But so much greater is the number who,
By nature, simply do not hesitate…
Then rushing forward, do what they must do,
And any hurt and harm alleviate.

Our future has such hope and joy to share,
Knowing these better Angels will be there.

34

The sun was slow in rising here today…
It seemed the moon refused to let it in;
Perhaps there was resentment in the way
The sun leaves little trace of where moon's been.

I've wondered could there ever be a rift
Between opposing forces in the sky?
Accepting each one brings our world a gift…
To choose a favorite, who'd even try?

For if the moon should ever cease to be,
The ocean tides would flow beyond their space;
Heaven forbid the sun would be set free,
Because quite soon life here would be erased.

I guess the lesson then for me to learn:
Shine brightly where I'm placed… and take my turn!

35

The old dog had been faithful for so long,
Staying quite near the one who called him friend…
And never went away when things went wrong,
He hoped the life he knew would never end.

He seemed to have keen insight all his own,
Full knowing when to go and when to stay;
Believing master's love for him had grown,
Brought joy and gladness to him every day!

One morning when his master called his name,
As always, he was quick to find his place;
But soon he realized things weren't the same,
Sensing such sadness on his master's face.

The old man, leaving, said in somber tone,
"With my friend near - I'll never be alone!"

36

High on a hill, some waited for that train…
Bright promises had somehow slipped away,
Accepting they had been misled again,
Sad future theirs, beginning here today.

So there they sat, recounting every dream,
That trip to Glory was their ticket out…
Now realizing things aren't what they seemed,
So little now to even dream about.

But even though He did not come as planned,
For even Angels do not know the date.
And promises of men are shifting sand…
He won't come early, nor will He come late.

Those folks caught up in fables now must see,
He will return, His time is yet to be.

37

There was a song His meadow sang each day,
Made up of pinks and yellows, golds and blues…
Warm breezes sifted colors on the way,
Beyond its borders, as the breeze will do.

Then, as it blended fragrance of the sounds,
The flowers weaving, waving to the tune…
Idyllic as the wildlife that is found,
Basking in the warm loveliness of June.

He placed a stream beside the forest there,
Quite softly it meandered past the trees…
All creatures drank cool water it would share,
Refreshing each and every one of these.

His Eden was a part of all He planned…
Where Nature sang the wonders of His hands!

38

A story that was told me long ago
About a man's encounter with a mouse...
The problems started small but then would grow,
Because the rodent sneaked into his house!

The critter ran inside the wall and hid,
Took over then as if it were his own,
Annoyed the man with mousy things it did,
Not long until annoyances had grown.

Quite helplessly the man searched for a cure...
Seemed nothing that he did would lure it out;
So hard, the pain the man had to endure,
The mouse was winning, beyond any doubt.

In desperation, one last thing he tried,
He fed his guest so well it could not hide!

39

Spring puts soft colored blossoms in her hair,
Then whispers closing words of Winter's song...
Reminds the cold there's no more time to share,
And for a while, it's best it moves along.

All Nature then will raise its sleepy head
To give the songbirds each their sweetest note,
To sing where streams of blissfulness are fed...
The greatest music His hand ever wrote.

Come night, new fawn will sleep on silken grass,
The doe is bathed in moonlight as they rest;
Another day of grandeur soon will pass...
The robin is returning to her nest.

There is a world that's waiting to be found...
Where times of restoration do abound!

40

There was a place, a dreary place it was,

Where gray clouds blocked all sunshine from the sky;

No color there to do what color does,

Soon folks forgot the reasons they should try.

The birds would just sit silently in trees…

They could not find a melody to sing,

As sadness stilled the song in each of these,

Then left them there with nothing else to bring.

But one day when the leader of that place

Sat silently, as most days would begin,

A butterfly came by to kiss his face,

As others watched him grin from cheek to chin!

Then magically came colors and a song!

Seems laughter they were missing all along.

41

It was a city built of wood, I'm told,
Each house and building made of fallen trees;
Most structures still around from days of old,
With woodsy fragrance carried on the breeze.

The people of the town tried hard to be
Quite open-minded to include all things…
Then daily looked for new ways they could see
What gifts their inclusivity could bring.

So, one day these kind folks were made aware
Termite families cried *discriminate*,
Complained and said the people didn't care,
And claimed it proved the termites didn't rate.

Woke residents soon let the termites in…
Then watched death from inclusiveness begin.

42

When beauty fades into a memory,
And when your body begs for still more rest...
When distant days are far too far to see,
And life is more a challenge than a quest.

When Autumn became Winter and you knew
The simple things weren't simple anymore...
Close friends now whittled down to just a few,
And losing them seems a revolving door.

Though age has taken much too much, we know...
Our life together, blessed since first we met,
We've way too many treasures now to show,
We're grateful for the ones still coming yet.

You've been my friend, my lover from the start...
You are indeed the true love of my heart!

43

The politician made his promise clear,

His dam most certainly would form a lake,

Then folks would come to see from far and near…

Think of what a difference it could make!

So grandiose their plans would come to be;

The people framed their fortunes far ahead,

As water rose to cover every tree,

Exactly as the politician said.

But later, when the people realized

Their little town was bursting at its seams…

The population grew to twice its size,

Growth problems quickly melted every dream.

Regrets came, as regrets will often do,

When people see their fantasies come true.

44

He sat beside the water for a bit,
Deciding should he go or should he stay…
While making up his mind, he chose to sit
And let the ripples take his cares away.

While half asleep, he heard a buzzing sound,
Providing him a welcomed, pleasant hunch;
He'd wait there for the fly to come around,
And yep, you guessed it, that would be his lunch!

So little there to keep a frog amused,
Each morning turns to afternoon then night;
So difficult for him to get enthused,
He won't get wet, but then again, he might.

Like many folks, he's learned to be content,
Waiting there and wondering where life went.

45

No one knows for sure just how it started,

As no one claimed to know how it began,

The pain it brought with problems uncharted,

By targeting the value of a man.

Seemed to float upon the air forever,

Just waiting on the chance to mark and maim,

Never took a break from that, no never,

In waves of needless hurt and harm it came!

Such is power of an innuendo,

It has no form or fabric to reveal…

Like unseen cancer cells, how it does grow,

Creating wounds that sometimes never heal.

Beyond all doubt a word can surely be

What holds a heart in chains, or sets it free!

46

It surely was the greatest time we'd had,
Our many hopes and dreams were coming true;
Old memories we'd cast aside were sad…
We were ready to make again, anew.

Trying hard to build on dreams of Eden,
Where time alone could make dark shadows fall;
To feel the feel of pleasant breeze again…
In short, this new place surely had it all.

Then we learned our plans were all mistaken,
For what we found was clearly far from good;
Empty plates of gold when food's been taken,
Then nothing's left to fill you as it should.

Caught up we were in this, life's cruel joke,
As we were gathered in the *land of woke*.

47

Why do we have to go so far away
To find grand things so many lives long for...
Not seeing treasures we pass every day,
It seems what's near is easy to ignore.

We yearn for places where we've never been,
Believing every step will be worthwhile;
Challenging distant space we find again
That many foreign customs aren't our style.

But still we keep on traveling ahead,
To see those sights from books and magazines...
Then marvel they're exactly as we've read,
Exchanging time for photographs we've seen.

Then while we're mesmerized by every frame,
Those folks are over here doing the same!

48

They ate the fruit and that's where it began,
Their downward spiral so out of control…
Affecting generations left to man,
Their actions brought them shallowness of soul.

No longer would fair Eden be their place,
The beauty of their past a memory…
With streams of perspiration on each face,
Thorns and thistles as far as they could see.

But even though their lives were torn apart,
Familiar now with work and pain and strife…
His mercy showed such love within His heart,
By placing them beyond the tree of life.

Man's hope for Paradise was not the same…
That is, until the *second Adam* came.

49

He whistles every night as he walks through,
Lifting the evening silence with his song…
He stares ahead as fearful men will do,
While praying none behind him sing along.

He always takes the shortcut past our door,
Although the path around would not add much,
It seems that saving steps for him is more
Important than dark shadows, sounds and such.

He never stops or even slows a bit…
I hear his coins that jingle as he goes,
As if his courage grows because of it;
A cemetery's chill, I know he knows.

But even if he doesn't see *us* near,
His *passing* always will be welcomed here.

50

Out there among the flowers and the trees

A meadow waits where quiet beauty lives,

A crystal stream brings nourishment to these

By always taking far less than it gives.

No mortal's recent steps upon the trails,

Made for the gentle creatures in its trust…

Extending little thought to life's details,

Which burden folks as though it seems they must.

But is there treasure in what's not been seen,

Is there intrinsic value wasting there…

Is beauty lost where man's not lately been,

Can *precious* describe something never shared?

So, did God in His wisdom have a plan:

Keep Eden for Himself long after man.

51

There are so many people big and small,
Each rushing to the place they want to go…
I've wondered how God ever sees them all,
Or manages to know the things they know.

I stand here watching as each life unfolds…
Like maps where no two places are the same;
With traits and talents, faiths and fears untold,
While many want to question why they came.

But finite is the mind of mortal man,
I have to pause to realize what's real…
God simply does it all because He can…
It makes no difference what we think or feel.

Perhaps He wonders why man stumbles here,
His caring nature really is quite clear.

52

Something I am beyond what folks can see,
Way down beneath my bones, blood and sinew…
Where soul and spirit form the part of me
That can't be seen by mortals, me and you.

My friends and relatives all know my face,
Can maybe even recognize my voice…
But, I'm referring to a deeper place
Where sight and touch and hearing aren't a choice.

For what can we identify of man,
Beyond the attributes they let us know…
Invisible, appears to be God's plan
To rarely let the real us ever show.

Perhaps when life here is all said and done,
True *us* will be reflections of the Son.

53

The barn was barely standing, I recall…
The roof and floor surrendered long ago,
Providing no resistance then at all
To rain and snow when bitter winds would blow.

When I left home as boys so often do,
To find the place where life would carry me;
Behind me were those simple things I knew…
That barn became a faded memory.

But in its day, it was my closest friend,
Long hours in its loft upon the hay…
I'd dream my dreams that seemed to have no end,
Until time took that little boy away.

While true we can't go back to where we've been…
Nostalgia can bring it to life again!

54

Here is my story best I can recall,
With me and Duley fishin in the creek…
The fish weren't biting, no, nothing at all,
When Duley looked my way and tried to speak.

I had just cast my jig when he began
A dancing, yelling words that were not clear;
Such sounds I'd never heard come from a man…
(I wondered if the devil found him here!)

I didn't know if I should stay or run,
For Duley was sure putting on a show;
I figured fishin for the day was done…
I thought if I could catch him, then we'd go.

Now Duley wasn't friendly, not a speck…
He blamed me for the jig stuck in his neck!

55

The picture lady rarely missed a shot,
Her camera was always set to go;
She knew just when and where to find the spot…
Amazing trophies she would have to show.

At every party, she would sure be there,
To capture every memory and smile…
Approaching every scene with loving care,
So graceful in the shadows all the while.

How many she's collected, who could guess,
Those countless boxes marked with place and year.
Such masterpieces, each one made to bless,
But has no time to look at them, I fear.

Perhaps when she is older, she will find
A chance to pause, to enjoy what's behind.

56

I bought myself an elephant one day
So big and gray and nimble on his feet…
What I would do with him I couldn't say,
Just owning him would make my life complete!

I realized my house was lacking space,
I built a room just to accommodate;
How happy he was there in his new place…
But then, I learned how much my new guest ate.

I work two jobs now just to pay his bills.
(I rarely see my elephant at all.)
I've spent so much it really gives me chills…
And which owns whom… no longer seems my call.

Men buy the things they see and then assume
Their elephant will always fit the room.

57

Riding the wind it came from who knows where,

Tied by a ribbon with a fancy touch…

Out on my walk, I found the pieces there;

At first, it really didn't seem like much.

I briefly paused to take a closer look…

A flat balloon, just laying on the grass;

I picked it up, and off the dampness shook.

I thought how nearly in my haste, did pass.

So clearly what I held there in my hands,

A testament to love some others shared…

Who launched this message to an unknown land,

Words from those left behind who clearly cared.

I would their grief abated as it soared,

As hearts reached out to heal, in one accord.

58

We get so busy doing what we do…

We work, we play, we face the storms and strife;

As time sends mysteries without a clue,

We sail upon this journey we call *life*.

Some folks are fortunate and find a friend,

Perhaps a lover as they move along;

The young believe their days will never end…

The old seek ways to tell them they are wrong.

And so the story goes and goes and goes…

The blessed may leave a mark on where they've been,

But realize that only Heaven knows

If they will ever pass this way again.

The wise hold fast to knowing time won't stall,

By living every day above it all.

59

Sit here and listen to the sound of wind,
It quickly moves across our Country's face…
Like promises that never seem to end,
Then quickly disappear without a trace.

Historians and talking heads agree,
Watch this phenomenon every four years!
Such pageantry and pompousness we see;
Such pageantry and pompousness we hear.

Real palpable excitement some folks find,
The cheering crowds, the waving flags and songs…
Some quickly leave all common sense behind,
Like lemmings moving rhythmically along.

After a while, the wind will shift away…
So little changes, and the sky's still gray.

60

I heard the song of robins and I knew
The golden sunlight woke them from their sleep…
For winter's closing serenade was through,
Now finally, spring's joy was ours to keep.

I'm sure there is good reason for the cold,
Else why would God have made it to be so?
I'll wait until someday that story's told…
Just add it to the things I'd like to know.

For seasons come and go, based on a plan…
So much of life we know is quite the same;
Earth's stage and scenery, set apart for man,
Move in precision since the day we came.

The sun, the stars, the moon, the air and more…
How could we ever doubt who they're here for?

61

I cannot help but wonder why it's so,
Some people seem to live beyond their time…
In barren, broken bodies when they know
Existence has no reason and no rhyme.

They've seen their spirit anchored to a chair
Or bed that long ago meant they would stay;
Bright eyes of yesterday a cloudy stare
To ask how *living* stole their life away.

I watch the mortal angels serving here,
Those gentle ones who tend to every need,
That try to make each patient's hope more clear
And mitigate each passing hour's greed.

But though the system seems to function well…
I'd gladly forfeit years, best I can tell.

62

If they had kept their promises to them,
This story, as we know it, might have changed;
Their vessels filled with deceit to the brim,
Their cruel intentions always were the same.

Our ancestors played on naïveté,
Used beads and trinkets as a currency…
Took more advantage each and every day,
While preaching how the Lord sets all men free.

America is certainly the best…
Our blessings flow beyond our wildest dreams;
It makes me wonder how we've been so blessed,
If recompense is close to what it seems.

Those times were very long ago, and yet…
It's fitting that we never do forget!

63

Just one more day with everything the same…
Repetitive is what my life is now.
There isn't really anyone to blame,
And who would I complain to anyhow?

There's not much anyone can do or say
To breathe new life into this one I've got;
I've heard the Lord is coming back someday…
I wonder why some others think He's not.

But somewhere in my mundane life I found
A tiny flower pushing through the sod,
There celebrating life in sun-caked ground,
Raising its face as giving praise to God.

Never again will I let anything
Deprive me of the joy that Hope can bring!

64

A story I was told from long ago
About a local beauty who had died
A hundred years before… but as we know,
Time often helps such storied facts to slide.

Her raven hair in curls beneath the glass,
Her cheeks were flushed, her lips were ruby red;
Reports from those who knew her when she passed
Agreed she certainly did not look dead.

The story culminates as locals then,
Years later, planned to move her quietly;
While peering through her coffin glass, her skin
Was perfect as an angel's there would be.

But people being people had to touch…
Air quickly erased her remnants as such.

65

Fair Heaven is an awesome place I'm sure,
With peaceful pleasures waiting there no doubt,
And crystal streams of water cool and pure,
And golden streets we've heard so much about.

So Lord, forgive me asking this one thing,
If, in Your mercy, You could make it be
That every dog I've ever owned You'd bring
To have them waiting for me by a tree.

The Collie and the Labrador, and then
The full menagerie of my old friends…
Imagine all the fun we'll have there when
We realize our summer never ends!

Lord, one more ask to make it all complete;
A cat or two to chase would be a treat!

66

A meteor brightened the midnight sky,
In glowing streaks of purple, pink and red…
So mesmerized by such a sight that I,
Sensed my imagination being fed.

It may be older than the earth we love,
And traveled distance we can't comprehend;
Perhaps beyond all we can see above
To where the universe begins to end.

I paused then, just to briefly give a thought
Of the places this traveler has been…
Then maybe did more dreaming than I ought
Until reality touched me again.

Exploding rock that traveled from afar,
Helps me to realize how small we are.

67

When I consider all the parts of me,
That myriad mass of nerves, cells and such…
With everything we can and cannot see,
Providing us with sight and sound and touch.

I pause to watch a newborn, and I know
Few can explain the things that it can do;
Its tiny arms and legs put on a show,
While eyes and voice express their point of view.

It simply is a miracle some say,
The way each part contributes to the whole…
Uniquely similar in its own way
To binding human spirit to the soul.

Each person must decide the path Man came,
But doubting God is folly just the same.

68

I'm sure there's something I came here to get…
I guess that's why I'm at the grocery store;
Apparently, quite easy to forget,
And have I ever been in here before?

Of late, my memory has missed a beat…
I walk into a room and wonder why,
Then pick up something else as I retreat;
This is just how my days go flying by.

It's clear that this *old house* is failing fast,
My hearing's shot, I guess my eyes are too;
I have my doubts my plumbing's gonna last.
The trains I've failed to catch, more than a few.

I'd gladly go and start over again…
My problem is recalling where I've been!

69

If every problem in the world was solved,
And life was blissful, way beyond compare,
If all the folks with attitudes evolved
Into kind people, full of love to share…

If poverty were suddenly erased,
If social status was then whisked away,
If every dream that everyone had chased
Were suddenly reality today…

But short of Heaven, how can these things be?
Aren't some folks far beyond redemption's sphere?
Is it folly to think the world could see
Beauty flourishing in our lives down here?

In darkness yet He shines His perfect light,
Welcomes transition from this great good night ….

70

One day the moon sent notice to the sun,

Considering their long-time harmony…

Said, "When I'm finished, your day's just begun,

For eons now, that's how it had to be."

"You live on your bright throne there in the sky,

While people *ooh* and *aah* about your place,

As though a simple afterthought am I,

A chunk of rock who has a friendly face."

"But now I'm tired of playing number two;

I plan to strike out on my own tonight…

I'm certain I can do the things you do;

I'll *make*, instead of *reflecting* the light!

The sun just smiled at all the moon had said…

Such danger when delusions fill our heads.

71

The rock was ancient, never was a doubt,
Just setting half-exposed atop the bluff…
A small, inviting shelf protruded out,
That stony stool for me was quite enough.

I'd sit for hours wrapped in solitude…
The river far below was quite a scene;
In innocence, a gray squirrel might intrude,
Confused by what my being there could mean.

A grown-up world then called me from my place;
Excitement clearly got the best of me.
I couldn't wait to join the human race,
And soon my rock became a memory.

So hard to measure just where it began…
The rock, the river, *fathers to the man.*

72

I have a snapshot in my mind from when
The circus came, those very special days…
The tents, the trapeze and the tigers then
Each did its best to push mundane away.

The show was quite spectacular to see,
Three rings of unbelievably neat stuff;
Just when we thought no wilder thing could be,
The next act would excite us, sure enough!

Clowns were always favorites, I recall,
Their antics seemed to made the show complete;
With stunts to make us laugh, they had them all,
They kept each thrilled and spellbound in our seat.

But what we did not know of clowns they sent…
Their *offspring* soon would run our government!

73

My memories come back like yesterday,
My grandma came, so folks could take a break;
She always took us young'uns out to play,
And we looked forward to the fun we'd make!

That day we romped and ran around the house…
I found myself alone, back in the yard;
I watched it slither, quiet as a mouse…
I don't believe I ever screamed so hard!

Well, Grandma quickly ran and fetched her hoe,
We always kept one right behind the door;
She said it was the devil, don't you know…
Then smiled and said, "He won't scare you no more!"

I saw him hacked and hanging in a tree,
How can he still be here bothering me?

74

Hollywood makes the Old West seem so real,
With cowboys standing tall like human gods,
Their blazing guns that always closed the deal,
White hats would always even up the odds.

Most arguments were settled in the street…
High noon is what they'd have us to believe,
Where good guys and the bad guys there would meet,
Unmitigated justice to receive.

Though history does not support those tales,
It seems some folks just cannot get their fill;
It does them good to see the good prevail,
Full knowing guys with black hats never will!

While in that world, the heroes never fall…
Truth is, it wasn't like that, not at all.

75

Now, once again it's time to say goodbye…
I've noticed that the evening's on its way;
The sun is setting in the Western sky,
And night will soon be pushing out the day.

I hope our journey was for you worthwhile,
With myriad diversions you could find,
That gave you pause, or even made you smile,
While briefly leaving *here and now* behind.

Truth is, it surely has been fun for me
To share my thoughts with you in gentle rhyme,
Like friends who sit to share a cup of tea
Then find ourselves just losing track of time…

A hug, or handshake just before I go,
Perhaps we'll meet again, I do hope so!

About the Author

Jim Shields has published numerous poetry and children's books. He lives in Lexington, KY, with his wife of 55 years. He enjoys spending time with his family, including two children and five grandchildren.

His books can be reviewed at JimShieldsAuthor.com

His e-mail: JimShieldsAuthor@Gmail.com